Affirmations & Positive Quotes

Part 1: Duality

From Within

Divine Feminine

Written by:

Falisha Hall

"From within Divine Feminine"

To be
Awake

Is to know thy neighbor

To be

Aware

Is to know thy self

"From within Divine Feminine "

Always
Shine light on the darkness.
Be Firm
set healthy boundaries.
Be Kind
but never be a pushover

Love

Is a nest, not a cage.

Be Safe, Be good, Be Wise.

"From Within Divine Feminine "
Your
Perception illustrates
Either
how ignorant or how wise you are

"From within Divine Feminine

Accepting being alone doesnt Make you lonely It Makes you self sufficient

To be bound

Is to be enslaved

To be connected

Is to be in love

"From Within Divine Feminine

As within, so Without...
As You
Find your power within
You
Leave your enemies without

Control your power
Reacting out of Truth
Brings good karma
Reacting out of Emotion
Brings bad karma

"From Within Divine Feminine "

Give a helping hand
But
never make someone feel as though you

have to do anything for them
Because

YOU DO NOT

"From within Divine Feminine "

Once you answer the call the process of transformation will began

How you handle the darkness, demons, trials & tribulations

Will determine if you will be Chosen

The key is to keep an Open Heart

"From within Divine Feminine "
Solitude
has taught me to accept myself in
its
Entirety

"From Within Divine Feminine "

Don't ever mistake my

Enthusiasm

For being

Naive

The death may be hard, dark & lonely
But when the

Rebirth & Acceptance

Is complete, there is a sense of

Peace & Protection

That no man can shake

"From Within Divine Feminine"

Trust the process, Stay Positive, Hold Your faith

"From Within Divine Feminine"

Instead of Saying,

"You have a cold"

Try saying,

"I'm getting over a cold"

-Two different "Intentions"

"From Within Divine Feminine"

I am
Wise,
Before I am enything else

"From Within Divine Feminine"

You can no longer accumulate wealth
From my Spiritual Ignorance

"Wisdom"
is the new
"Power"

"From Within Divine Feminine"

Do not mistake my
"Free Spirit"
For being easy accessible

When you consistently apply

"Pressure"

It becomes Impossible to fold under it

"From Within Divine Feminine"

You will never find me where you left me

"Evolution"

Is Infinite, Limitless & Unbound

Don't ever mistake my

Enthusiasm

For being easily

Accessible

"From within Divine Feminine"

Being Spiritually dumb is not cool

I will Forever be

Spiritually, Emotionally, Physically, &

Financially Wise

Now that's cool....

"From Within Divine Feminine"

Awa"K"e – To Know

Awa"R"e – To Remember

Learn to discern the difference between:

"illusion" Of your Desires

-Vs-

"Fulfillment" Of your Desires

"From Within Divine Feminine"

Things I am
Thankful For:
Life & Death, Evolution, Spirituality
The Presence of God, True love, Self love,
Patience, Inner Peace, Discernment &
Truth

Having a one track mind

is the

Epitome

Of ignorance

"From Within Divine Feminine"

It's Time to do better Because

We are better &

We Know

Better

"From Within Divine Feminine"

What a man does for me
does not determine my Value
What I can & will do for myself
holds
great value

"From Within Divine Feminine"

Knowledge
Is found in books

Wisdom
Is found in experience

"From Within Divine Feminine"

To know the differnce between
god's laws &

Man's laws

Is to be wise…

living on
"Angel Time"
Is much more fulfilling

To be written
In a book is
Man's Work
To be written
In the stars is
Gods Work

"From Within Divine Feminine"

Instead of Saying,
"People fear what they dont Innerstand"

Try Saying,
"People use to fear what they Don't Innerstand"

"Two different Intentions

"From Within Divine Feminine"

To be mindless
Is to be Incompetent
To be Incompetent
Is to be Ignorant

Ignorance is not bliss....

"From Within Divine Feminine"

Not cocky,
But...
Spiritually Confident
With a heart of gold
&
Mind of Power

"From Within Divine Feminine"

forgiveness

Is for me NOT you & it does

not mean I will allow

you back in my energy

to harm me

"The lesson was learned"

"Fear"

Is one energy I'll never sit with

"From Within Divine Feminine"

I don't wanna be cocky,
I wanna be Solid.

Physically, Emotionally, Financially &
Spiritually "Solid"

"From Within Divine Feminine"

Gospel music & Praise music

guve different vibes

Gospel
Gives past.

Praise
Gives future.

"From Within Divine Feminine"

Metaphysical-

A reality beyond human

perception...

"From Within Divine Feminine"

If you don't innerstand what being

Unapologetically

Free means

Step into the Spiritual realm

We Are funny up here

"From Within Divine Feminine"

A King leading an Empress is Wild...

Come to me in your Emperor Energy
If you have any intentions of
leading me
This means Emotionally, Spiritually,
Physically & Financially balanced

Acting as if you don't <u>Innerstand</u>

What I'm saying

Will end a conversation

As long as you can read **Between** Words

I will have a conversation with **You**

"From Within Divine Feminine"

Once you've been Battle tested

You've officially become

Allie Status

When it's Him For me

It's a "Hard No"

For every body else

Physically "Awake"

Spiritually "Aware"

To have the best of

both worlds

Is to be limitless

If your experiences
Have made you *Bitter*
Then you have
Learned
Nothing...

"From Within Divine Feminine"

Experiences
Should make you better
Not
Bitter

And I really don't wanna sound

Conceded.

But...

I'm the type of woman

You need to be with

Love
is an energy I will always
And
Forever
Embody

"From Within Divine Feminine"

When your passion matches your
Lifestyle

It's guaranteed to bring

Success

If you're not Mentally or Spiritually stable

Then your Physical or Financial status

Means nothing to

Me

"From Within Divine Feminine"

I don't mind taking healthy risks,

It's the **Unnecessary** Risks

That dont sit well with me

Recording sexual activities is for the birds

I want my companion so engaged

Into what we're doing

That privacy is

"Imperative"

"From Within Divine Feminine"

1st & 2nd base in High School is wild.
Now & days you have to have the mental
Capacity to hold a Conversation
With me to even be
Considered
For a date

Mastered
the art of detachment
Now,
I'm working on my health

"From Within Divine Feminine"

Expand your horizon:
Obtain both Wisdom & Knowledge
Knowledge from books.
Wisdom from experience
They are both learning tools & navigation
manuals for the
Human Experience

Don't expect me to curve me enthusiasm

To please your

Beliefs

I am a

Multi-Faceted

Being

"From Within Divine Feminine"

I lack

Nothing...

Her words soothe
The souls of the ones
Unheard

"From Within Divine Feminine"

Its
You
Vs
You...
Your higher Self
Vs
Your Lower Self

"From Within Divine Feminine"

Chin up,
Chest out,
Feet
"grounded"

Wrote in the stars
And I'm Lucky
So I pray through it

"From Within Divine Feminine"

"Self love"
Is
Essential

"From Within Divine Feminine"

Let's make it a

"Lifestyle"

Get Fit

"From Within Divine Feminine"

To be bound is to live in Slavery

To be connected is to live in Love

Free your Mental Space

Do not become the people who hurt you
But become the Leader the
People who hurt you look up to.

"From Within Divine Feminine"

One of the
Healthiest things
You can do is
Express Yourself

Getting started is half the battle

Consistently

Showing up is

The other half

"From Within Divine Feminine"

When you've Evolved from

"Queen" To "Empress"

You've reached

Self Mastery

I choose to Inspire
Climbing the ladder to my
highest Desires

"From Within Divine Feminine"

To win the game you have to
Think bigger,
See clearer,
Move Swifter
To escape the unseen forces
That work against you

You must reclaim your name

From a bad energy Exchange

It's not where you've been, But

Where you wanna go that changes the

Game

"From Within Divine Feminine"

To Overcome is to gain

Mastery

Over your lower self

"From Within Divine Feminine"

Be mindful of your energy

Exchange

It's a energy

Game !!

Don't expect me to dance around the truth
As if I cant see, feel or hear
With the
Swiftness,
I am gifted !!

"From Within Divine Feminine"

I am free.
Unapologetically Free to be me
I am in control of my emotions
You see,
This means I stand
In my power fully

"From Within Divine Feminine"

I respectfully Respect everyone
On a soul level.

This is what
Protects
Me

Generational Curse Breaker.

Shaking the world up

like a salt shaker.

When vibrating high,

She's

Beautiful & Desirable,

Impeccable & Admirable.

SoulTies combine & Intertwine
like weeds in a Garden

Some for growth,
Some to Pardon

Twin Flame or Soulmate
Both can be Karmic depending on
Your Intuition &
How you discern it.

Lush of the flesh is a weak man's trait

When you slay that Dragon

You will see heavens gate.

"From Within Divine Feminine"

Strength, Roots & Logic
Makes him a Divine Masculine

Learning not to be
Toxic

Love is Infinite, love is bold.

Love is the greatest gift

Man could ever hold.

The mind is beautiful yet
So mysterious, connected to divinity
Has everyone
Curious

"From Within Divine Feminine"

The Spiritual Journey teaches you
a lot about life, gaining much
Insight
On the wrong & right

"From Within Divine Feminine"

When God is in it,
There is no
Limit

Distance makes the heart grow fonder.
While enemies at play
Make the bond even
Stronger

"From Within Divine Feminine"

Divine Masculine must surrender to the love
Divine Feminine has to offer for
Divine Feminine To summit to letting
Divine Masculine
Lead

"From Within Divine Feminine"

I am
Multi-
Dimensional

My love is the only drug you need.

It'll take as high as the Heavens

Have you ever been high off Life

"From Within Divine Feminine"

Soul-Family,
We look for energy,
Not
Imagery

When you can discern "**Heaven Sent**"
From "Devil Sent" you can start
To accumulate assets
Not liabilities

I am grateful
For all things
That are
Good

I intentionally distribute good energy

For my offspring to inherit

Good Karma

Father God, I am grateful for everything That you have done for me & for everything You are about to do for me.

From Within Divine Feminine

I am Complex

But......

I am Simplicity

This is Duality

Masculine & Feminine,

Good & Bad,

Light & Dark

"Which makes me an Unstoppable force to be reckoned with."

www.ingramcontent.com/pod-product-compliance
Lightning Source LLC
Chambersburg PA
CBHW042132150726
48005CB00028B/778